Modelling Figures in

Simple Animals.

Modelling figures in clay. Volume1.

Simple Animals.

Introduction.

This is the first volume in our 'Clay Modelling Series.

The animals contained in the book were developed over the years and have been used to introduce basic clay modelling skills in school children of all ages. The figures are built up from simple shapes to which the students can relate.

Each project is demonstrated step by step as you work through the text, this is the technique we developed and found most effective over the years, and the objective of each step of the project is shown in the still photos. The step by step approach allows teachers to control the pace of the exercise, helping slower pupils at each stage and handing out the next piece of clay when **all** the pupils are ready.

The most important sheet in each project is the **'Worksheet'** which contains the weight of clay and the templates required to ensure the correct proportions of the models.

Each project has an element of decision making and measurement built into the worksheet with self expression encouraged in the decoration and design details applied to each model which becomes an individual creation.

Used regularly the projects will turn Teachers and Classroom Assistants into experienced modellers in clay. Repeated exposure to the techniques will encourage school staff to design and expand in-house projects. The keys are the weights, dimensions, and shapes. See **'Thirty Steps to Clay Modelling'** for further information which outlines all the basic skills needed for successful clay modelling projects.

Preparation.

The Worksheet should be made available to each work group to allow them access to the templates, we have found that one sheet to four children is a good balance.

As the sheet can come into contact with wet clay it is recommended that the master is copied and each sheet is sleeved or laminated to avoid clay smudges. Once the sheets are covered they can be kept for repeated sessions and become a school resource.

When we worked with groups the clay was prepared prior to the session.

Preparation consisted of weighing out the pieces and sealing clay for a specific purpose in a plastic bag to keep it moist.

Enjoy Your Clay Modelling.

Clay Modelling Tools.

All the tools can be bought in craft or hobby shops or you can produce cheap alternatives which are just as good and in some cases better and more suitable for use in schools.

Modelling tools shown are the simple tools needed for sculpting small models, most thumb pots and most coil pots.

The paint brush is chosen for its stiff bristles which allow you to rough up the clay to help with cross hatching or obviate the need for cross hatching in some circumstances.

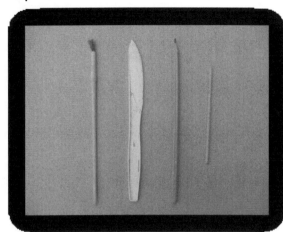

Plastic knives with the serrated edges trimmed using scissors and sharpened on sand paper are a cheap alternative to a potter's fettling knife and more suitable for use by young children. They are used primarily for cutting lengths of clay but can be used as a spatula to smooth joints between pieces of clay.

Pencils or pointed sticks, shown in the picture, are used for adding details such as eyes or hair to models or drawing patterns and designs on pots of all descriptions. The pointed stick shown was made from 3mm thick skewers used in cooking Kebabs. Cut the skewer to the length you need, I got three from one skewer, sharpen one end and round off the other end using sand paper.

The work surface shown is made from 4mm thick, three ply or MDF sheet and is 20cm x30cm.

These tools represent a one off purchase as a central resource for a school to be used by any class as required.

Modelling figures in clay.

Volume1. Simple Animals.

Contents.

Modelling Figures in Clay.

Simple Animals.

1. Hedgehog.

1. Hedgehog. 9

1. Hedgehog.

Roll a ball.

Roll the clay between the palms of your hands, exerting sufficient force to remove any lumps or bumps. Don't be tempted to take the easy route to smooth the clay by rolling it on the wooden work surface as this removes moisture from the clay and could make it too hard for modelling. Any creases or cracks can be smoothed using the fingers. Continue to roll the clay until the surface is smooth and the clay is the desired shape ie a ball shape.

Make an egg shape.

Take the clay ball between the palms of your hands and roll it into an egg shape. Roll the clay backwards and forwards across your palms exerting sufficient pressure to form the egg shape. The best way is to roll the clay a few times, check the shape then roll it a bit more, keep rolling and checking until you get the shape that you need. Complete the shape by rounding off the ends of the egg with your fingers.

Make a pointed nose.

The next part of the exercise is to form one end of the egg into a cone shape. This is done by using the fingers and thumb of one hand while holding the egg shape firmly in the other hand. Press and squeeze the clay between the fingers and thumb, turn the clay round a bit and press and squeeze again, repeat this until the cone shape shown in the picture is formed. Give the nose a smooth surface by sliding your fingers across the surface until it is smooth.

Eyes, nose, mouth and spikes.

With the pointed stick make two eyes and two ears. Use the point of the plastic knife to make the spikes, start above the eyes and cover the back and sides as shown in the picture, It is like drawing '1's all over his back. Take a tiny piece of clay and form a ball to use as the tip of the nose, rub water onto the top of the cone shape and on the ball to form slip, press the nose onto the cone. Finally draw a smiley mouth under the nose.

B & M POTTERYCRAFTS.

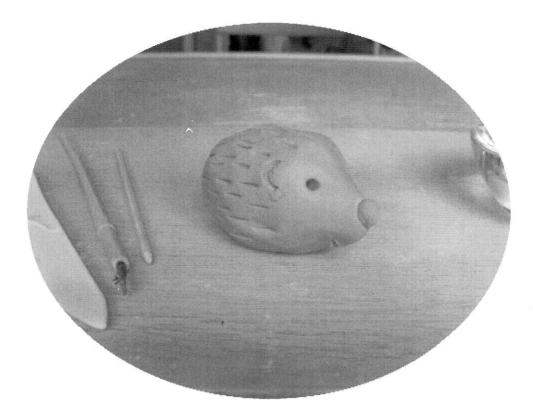

Worksheet. Hedgehog.

Clay.

Body.   80 grams

Nose.   Small piece.

B & M Potterycrafts.

Modelling Figures in Clay.

Simple Animals.

2. Mouse.

Sequence.

2. Make a Mouse.

Roll a ball.

Roll the clay between the palms of your hands, exerting sufficient force to remove any lumps or bumps. Don't be tempted to take the easy route to smooth the clay by rolling it on the wooden work surface as this removes moisture from the clay and could make it too hard for modelling. Any creases or cracks can be smoothed using the fingers. Continue to roll the clay until the surface is smooth and the clay is the desired shape i.e. a ball shape.

Make an egg shape.

Take the clay ball between the palms of your hands and roll it into an egg shape. Roll the clay backwards and forwards across your palms exerting sufficient pressure to form the egg shape. The best way is to roll the clay a few times, check the shape then roll it a bit more, keep rolling and checking until you get the shape that you need. Complete the shape by rounding off the ends of the egg with pressure from your fingers and thumbs.

Make a pointed nose.

The next part of the exercise is to form one end of the egg shape into a cone shape, the modelling is done by using the fingers and thumb of one hand while holding the egg shape firmly in the other hand. Press and squeeze the clay between the fingers and thumb, turn the clay round a bit and press and squeeze again, repeat this until the cone shape shown in the picture is formed. Give the nose a smooth surface by sliding your fingers across the surface until it is smooth.

Make eyes.

Use the pointed stick to make two holes to represent the eyes of the mouse.

Make and fit ears.

First make two slots to place the ears into by pressing the blunt end of the plastic knife into the clay as shown in the picture.

Next roll the clay into a ball and then into a short sausage shape, cut the sausage shape in half and roll the pieces into two balls. Squash these small balls in the palm of your hand with the thumb forming two discs. Dip the brush in water and rub the water firmly into the two slots to form **slip,** again with water on the brush make slip on one edge of each ear. Press the ears firmly into the hole, slip to slip.

The creation of **slip** is an important part of joining together two pieces of clay. The water from the brush is rubbed firmly into the clay surface until it turns light grey

The use of **pressure** is essential in successfully joining two pieces of clay when used in conjunction with crosshatching and slip.

Make and fit the tail.

Roll the clay into a smooth ball and then use the palms of your hands to roll a sausage shape to form the tail, use the template on the worksheet to check the correct length. With the brush and water make a line of slip on the mouse's back and also along the length of the tail. Press one end of the tail onto the mouse and stick the tail along his back as shown in the pictures.

Nose, mouth and whiskers.

Take a small piece of clay to make the tip of the mouse's nose, roll it into a ball, and by making slip on the ball and on the tip of the nose area fix the tip to the face.

Use the pointed stick to give the mouse a 'smiley mouth' and whiskers on each side of his face.

B & M Potterycrafts.

Make a mouse worksheet.

Clay.

Body. 80 grams.

Ears. 3 grams.

Tail.   3 grams.

Nose.   Small ball.

Tail template.   [   ]

B & M Potterycrafts.

Modelling Figures in Clay.

Simple Animals.

Ladybird.

B & M Potterycrafts.

Sequence.

3. Make a Ladybird.

Roll a ball.

Roll the clay between the palms of your hands, exerting sufficient force to remove any lumps or bumps. Don't be tempted to take the easy route to smooth the clay by rolling it on the wooden work surface as this removes moisture from the clay and could make it too hard for modelling. Any creases or cracks can be smoothed using the fingers. Continue to roll the clay until the surface is smooth and the clay is the desired shape i.e. a ball shape.

Create a half ball.

Having made the ball shape the next thing we have to do is to form the ladybird's body which is a hemisphere or a half ball shape.

The simple way to make a half ball is to throw the ball down, firmly, onto the wooden work surface. Take the clay in your hand, practice the throwing motion several times before throwing the clay down onto the board. This creates the half ball shape shown in the picture.

Make and fit the head.

Roll the clay into a smooth ball and, using the 'half ball' technique, make the head by throwing the ball firmly onto the board.

Refer to the **worksheet** to determine where the head is fitted to the body.

Use the knife point to crosshatch the head and the body where they fit together, this helps the clay to bond together.

Rub your paint brush and water firmly in the crosshatched areas to create slip on both pieces before pressing the head firmly onto the body.

The creation of **slip** is an important part of joining together two pieces of clay. The water from the brush is rubbed firmly into the clay surface until it turns light grey

Crosshatching is one of the keys to joining two pieces of clay. It consists of the scoring the pieces in the areas to be joined. Use the point of the knife to mark clay.

The use of **pressure** is essential in successfully joining two pieces of clay when used in conjunction with crosshatching and slip.

Make and fit the eyes.

Roll the clay into a short sausage and make a mark in the middle, when you are satisfied that the mark is in the middle cut the sausage in half.,

These two pieces are rolled into two balls and each one is thrown against the work surface to form 'half ball' eyes.

To fix the eyes, apply slip to the flat surface on each eye and on the head, crosshatching isn't needed to attach the smaller pieces.

Create face and wing case.

To create the design on the ladybird start with the wing case, use the pointed end of the wooden stick

Draw a line from the back of the head across the shell case right down to the end of the body. Don't use the point like a pencil because this scrapes clay from the body, the trick is to lay the point almost flat on the clay and drag the edge of the stick across the body, this technique gives a smoother line.

Use the rounded edge of the stick to make the spots on the ladybird's back. The pattern of dots on one side is mirrored on the opposite side that is the sides are 'symmetrical'.

To complete the ladybird we have to make the features, use the wooden stick to make two eyes, two nostrils and a smiley mouth.

B & M POTTERYCRAFTS.

Ladybird Worksheet.
Clay.

Body.   **80 grams.**

Head.   **5 grams.**

Eyes.   **Small piece.**

B & M Potterycrafts.

Modelling Figures in Clay.

Simple Animals.

Frog.

4. Make a Frog. **27**

4. Make a Frog.

Roll a ball.

Roll the clay between the palms of your hands, exerting sufficient force to remove any lumps or bumps. Don't be tempted to take the easy route to smooth the clay by rolling it on the wooden work surface as this removes moisture from the clay and could make it too hard for modelling. Any creases or cracks can be smoothed using the fingers. Continue to roll the clay until the surface is smooth and the clay is the desired shape ie a ball shape.

Make and fit feet.

Roll the clay into a ball and then into a short sausage shape. This helps with the next stage which is to cut the clay in half as it is easier to judge the centre of a sausage shape than the centre of a ball.

Roll the two pieces into two balls and gently squash each ball in the palm of one hand with the thumb of the other hand, check the size against the template on the worksheet.

Use the brush and water to create **slip.** Dip the brush in the water then firmly rub the brush across the clay on the body where the feet fit and also on the edge of the feet. **Press** the feet firmly onto the body and smooth the points under the frog where the feet fit the body, this makes the joint more secure.

Eyes.

As we did with the feet, roll the clay into a ball and then into a sausage shape which is cut in half to be used in making two eyes. Roll two balls to make the eyes, rub the brush with water on it in two spots on the top of the frog and make slip in both eyeballs, press the eyes firmly into place.

Finishing touches.

Use the point of the wooden stick to make two eyes and two nostrils. Again using the point draw a big 'smiley' mouth across the front of the frog. Finally use the point of the knife to give him three toes on each foot.

The creation of **slip** is an important part of joining together two pieces of clay. The water from the brush is rubbed firmly into the clay surface until it turns light grey this is the slip and act as our glue.

The use of **pressure** is essential in successfully joining two pieces of clay when used in conjunction with crosshatching and slip.

B & M Potterycrafts.

Frog. Worksheet.

Clay.

Body. 80 grams.

Feet.   15 grams.

Eyes.   5 grams.

Foot template.

B & M Potterycrafts.

Modelling Figures in Clay.

Simple Animals.

Rabbit.

5. Make a Rabbit. 32

5. Make a Rabbit.

Roll a ball.
Roll the clay between the palms of your hands, exerting sufficient force to remove any lumps or bumps. Don't be tempted to take the easy route to smooth the clay by rolling it on the wooden work surface as this removes moisture from the clay and could make it too hard for modelling. Any creases or cracks can be smoothed using the fingers. Continue to roll the clay until the surface is smooth and the clay is the desired shape ie a ball shape.

Make an egg shape.
Take the clay ball between the palms of your hands and roll it into an egg shape. Roll the clay backwards and forwards across your palms exerting sufficient pressure to form the egg shape. The best way is to roll the clay a few times, check the shape then roll it a bit more, keep rolling and checking until you get the shape that you need. Complete the shape by rounding off the ends of the egg with your fingers.

Make and fit the head.
Roll the clay into a smooth ball in the palms of your hands, when the ball is prepared give it two small rolls across your palms and it should turn into an egg

shape as shown in the picture.

With the point of the knife scratch the '#' sign on the head and on the body where the head is going to fit. This is called **crosshatching.** Dip the brush in water and rub the brush firmly across the crosshatch marks to create **slip,** this helps the clay bond together.

Press the head and body firmly together to fix the head.

Tail.

Use the wooden stick to make a mark at the back of the rabbit where the tail is going to fit.

Roll the small piece of clay into a smooth ball in the palms of your hands. With the brush and water make slip on one side of the tail and in the hole, press the tail firmly into place as shown on the picture.

Make and fit the ears.

Start by rolling the clay into a smooth ball then roll it into a sausage shape to the length shown on the worksheet.

When rolling the sausage shape try to keep it the same thickness all along the length.

Use your thumb to slightly squash the sausage from one end to the other as rabbit's ears are flat. Use the knife to cut this strip of clay in half to form the ears.

With water and the brush make slip on the back of the head and on the ears where they have been cut. Press the ears firmly onto the head as shown in the picture.

Eyes, mouth and nose.

With the little wooden stick make two holes for the eyes, remembering that rabbit's eyes are at the side of the head.

The mouth and nose are made at the same time by pressing the edge of the knife twice at the front of the head to form an 'X'. Pressing the knife into the clay rather than drawing with it has the effect of pushing up the clay at each side and forming the nose at the same time.

The creation of **slip** is an important part of joining together two pieces of clay. The water from the brush is rubbed firmly into the clay surface until it turns light grey

Crosshatching is one of the keys to joining two pieces of clay. It consists of the scoring the pieces in the areas to be joined. Use the point of the knife to mark clay.

The use of **pressure** is essential in successfully joining two pieces of clay when used in conjunction with crosshatching and slip.

Worksheet. Make a Rabbit.

Clay and Sequence.

Body.   80 grams.

Head.   10 grams.

Tail.   Small ball.

Ears.   5 grams.   ☐

Scale.   ☐   4 cms.

Important. Copy this sheet to scale.

B & M Potterycrafts.

Modelling Figures in Clay.

Simple Animals.

Duck.

Contents and sequence.

6. Make a duck.

Roll a ball.

Roll the clay between the palms of your hands, exerting sufficient force to remove any lumps or bumps. Don't be tempted to take the easy route to smooth the clay by rolling it on the wooden work surface as this removes moisture from the clay and could make it too hard for modelling. Any creases or cracks can be smoothed using the fingers. Continue to roll the clay until the surface is smooth and the clay is the desired shape ie a ball shape.

Make an egg shape.

Take the clay ball between the palms of your hands and roll it two or three times to make an egg shape. Roll the clay backwards and forwards across your palms exerting sufficient pressure to form the egg shape. The best way is to roll the clay a few times, check the shape then roll it a bit more, keep rolling and checking until you get the shape that you need. Complete the shape by rounding off the ends of the egg with your fingers.

Make and fit the head.

Roll the clay into a smooth ball in the palms of your hands. With the point of the knife scratch the # sign on the head and on the body where the head is going to fit. This is called **crosshatching.** Dip the brush in water and rub the brush firmly across the crosshatch marks to create **slip,** this helps the clay bond together.

Press the head and body firmly together to fix the head.

Make and fit the tail.

Roll the clay into a smooth ball and then squash it flat in the palm of the hand with the thumb of the other hand.

Use the handle of the plastic knife to make a slot to fit the tail into.

With the brush and water create slip in the slot and on one edge of the tail and press the tail firmly into the slot.

The creation of **slip** is an important part of joining together two pieces of clay. The water from the brush is rubbed firmly into the clay surface until it turns light grey this is the slip and act as our glue.

Crosshatching is one of the keys to joining two pieces of clay. It consists of the scoring the pieces in the areas to be joined. Use the point of the knife to score clay.

The use of **pressure** is essential in successfully joining two pieces of clay when used in conjunction with crosshatching and slip

Make and fit the beak.

The first job is to make a slot with the knife handle, as we did with the tail, but this time the slot is across the front of the head.

Start the beak by rolling the clay into a ball and then into a jellybean, cut the jellybean in half and roll the two pieces into two balls. Squash these balls slightly with the thumb of one hand on the palm of the other hand, to form the top and bottom parts of the beak. With the brush and water create slip in the slot by rubbing the brush firmly across the slot. Make slip on one edge of the lower part of the beak and press it into the slot sloping downwards as shown on the picture. Repeat this with the upper part of the beak but this time the beak slopes upwards.

Eyes and wings.

With the wooden stick make two holes for the eyes at the front of the head and draw the wing along each side of the body, refer to the picture if you are not sure of the positioning.

B & M Potterycrafts.

Worksheet.Make a Duck.

Clay and Sequence.

Body.   80 grams.

Head.   15 grams.

Tail.   3 grams.

Beak.   1 gram.

Printed in Great Britain
by Amazon.co.uk, Ltd.,
Marston Gate.